The Road To Paradise

by
André Taylor

authorHOUSE™
1663 LIBERTY DRIVE, SUITE 200
BLOOMINGTON, INDIANA 47403
(800) 839-8640
WWW.AUTHORHOUSE.COM

© 2005 André Taylor. All Rights Reserved.

No part of this book may be reproduced, stored in a retrieval system, or transmitted by any means without the written permission of the author.

First published by AuthorHouse 07/15/05

ISBN: 1-4208-6976-0 (sc)
ISBN: 1-4208-6975-2 (dj)

Printed in the United States of America
Bloomington, Indiana

This book is printed on acid-free paper.

Scripture Quotations: New King James Version (1999, Zondorvan)

Amplified Bible (1999, Zondervan)
Websters & The Oxford Dictionary used 1997
Back cover photo by Muchel Bocandé

Prologue

If you can change God, and conform Him by your opinion of who you think He is-what you think-He should be or do, then you become God. It is you who must be conformed to God's ways. The flesh, the natural man with all his desires, ideas and philosophies, must be broken before God as though dead. All knowledge that is written in a book is first experienced. The revelation, knowledge, and information in this book have come from a twenty year developmental process walking with God-through despair, incarceration, anxiety, failure, riches, lasciviousness, women, family, the church, the streets, visions, dreams, and the spirit. All were ordained by God for my development as a prophet. A prophet is a person God has chosen for a particular time in the earth, to speak or bring about God's will. Each one is the voice of God and normally each of them are hidden by a life that seems contrary to his calling. But when they are fully developed for their mission, God brings them out of their hiding place, to bring a vision, a word from God and judgement in the earth.

I dedicate this book to Eugene Morgan, who was the human angel God used to lighten my load through jail, prison, and probation. I love you Gene.

Thus saith the Lord, "It was I the Holy Ghost that touched Gene's heart and caused him to help you."

Acknowledgements

I express my love to my wife, Athena Taylor—no ifs, whats or maybes—she's the real thing from heaven. To my father Mel Taylor, who was reserved on verbal support, but with a love fully tilted in my favor, I admire you. To my family, and to my friends, who became family and brought support in times of despair, I bless you. To my editor, Nancy Padrón, who became my mother so that she could hear my voice with maternal ears, I love you. And to all those who, when faced with injustice, have the courage to be fair, when having the power to be otherwise, I honor you.

Chapter One: The Foundation

Endless years before coming home I had walked a path of broken footsteps, and my eyes told the story, and now I sit traveling through the ruins of my past. The light flickering close to its death seems to hypnotize me as I gaze at the pale painted walls that hug me in my jail cell. I remember having had this feeling once before rushing down the canal of my mother's womb, as my past flashed before me of nine months in solitary confinement anticipating something new. Only God and I knew the promises we had made to one another, so the humiliation associated with people pointing the finger at me, I knew, was for my cultivation. I had walked long enough as a caterpillar, but to become a butterfly there first has to be a cocoon; this jail cell was my cocoon. The cocoon comes after baptism by fire, the sprinkling of salt, and the walk as a caterpillar.

The steps along the pathway of my life were never self-explanatory, but they lured me with the promise of freedom. Life had been this way for me—a lesson within my failed attempts to find myself. Like in the first grade when I skipped school following after Carl, who was a little older than me and seemed to have a more fun. Not knowing my plight for fun and just being six years old kept me from the simple knowledge that is was policy for the school to call home when a student didn't show up.

I got the worst whipping that lasted so long it seemed to have carried a torch that marched on for many years. I knew from this incident that the consequences of my actions will never again be a substitute for the sole responsibility of being my own leader.

"Chow's on deck." I awoke startled by that consistent statement that was filled with a voice that changed everyday. I felt I heard that saying a thousand times in a day, and each day was a parallel line with forever. I knew that time stopped for no one, but it had a way of pacing itself when the passenger is in a jail cell. I thought about the other inmates-how they must feel-the ones that had never been to Hawaii and snorkeled in Honomu Bay swimming with blue, white, and yellow multicolored fish, or the congregation of Japanese tourists, the ones that had never been to Mardi Gras to see, the Zulu dancers the peacocks of the festival, the ones who could never say they blended in with the young and old dancing in a second line, and the ones who would never eat in Hollywood at the Dar Maghreb where there are Moroccan belly dancers who balance swords on their heads. At least I had my memories. They became so priceless I began to count them like money...a wealth of experience and riches of adventure. I thought about Jose, the little Mexican boy who had just been convicted of murder and was facing two life sentences. I couldn't even imagine the lifeless feeling of the only thing to look forward to are the days that pass.

This particular evening nightfall had an eerie tone and aggression was in the air. It was the weekend and we were all locked down in our cells without free time. The air was crowded with complaints and as the voices struggled for a leader, the air slowly freed itself. Two hours passed and the last voice faded into eleven o'clock, and by midnight, the sound of heavy sleep emanated from many jail cells. Resting on the rock of thought, I could feel the death of men's desires for another chance at freedom, and then I knew; that too late was the graveyard for untimely learners. My sleep that night was chartered with the good fortune of a traveler passing by disaster on his way home, and my striving to move forward was in agreement with forgetting the past, because the memory of my past pains resurrected the pain within me.

I remember the evening I died! I had battled passion

for three days by restraining myself from seeing Pam, but I was easily defeated by a fight that men never win. I met Pam when I was fifteen, and she was eighteen. She was America's ideal of perfect beauty. Her hair was blond, and highlighted to confirm the color. She had blue-green eyes that changed color according to her mood. Her body was fresh, like an idea in early America, and she had the kind of beauty that made others doubt their own.

This gave her confidence, favor, and the attitude, encouraged by white men, that all things are to be placed at her feet. I loved her and any girl before her I hated when compared to how I loved Pam, and only time would give me reason to love someone else more. My wanting Pam was two-fold; to have what white men most desired, and the revenge of conquering what they most praised. Pam and I would take walks together just to see who would get the most looks. She was my partner in conceit, and we understood each others vanity. She had experienced sex three other times before me, so it was me who traveled in and out of her entry doors, pounding open her walls until they would accommodate me without resistance. And it was she who, matching my aggression, surrendered her body a servant to please my passion. Our love was naked to the world and we never dressed it up; the picnics we had at Green Lake, the car rides we took, purposely getting lost, and the laughter we shared finding our way out, made turning sixteen with Pam all the more sweet. But the obstacle her mother and stepfather became was no match for rebellion and love, because resistance gave these two a reason to strive harder.

One of the greatest show of strength in a man is when he has looked into the eyes of an unfaithful woman he loves, imagining the sexual strokes of another man without breaking stride; without judging her. But a greater show of strength is that of a boy forming his identity, giving up the girl he feels is perfect, for something that has to be believed in before it's more rewarding. And that's how I met God-callous, no compromise, and no space for crying.

The preacher said that premarital sex was a sin; that Jesus died for my sins. He said I didn't have to believe him but I could read the Bible myself and find out how beautiful God is and how much he desires to make Himself real to me. As long as I can remember I've had within me a Divine peace and assurance that nothing life-threatening could ever happen to me. I understood then that this protection came from God, and a price came with it, and I was expected to pay for it with my life, and now the time had come.

In the beginning, my new found love for the knowledge of God was pursued equally between Pam and I. We went to church together, and were even excited about getting married so that we could add God's blessing to our perfect union. But when the preacher reminded us in a church meeting that premarital sex was a sin, Pam began to find reasons not to go to church anymore. She said the preacher was a racist and didn't want to see us together. She said she didn't mind going to an all black church, but sometimes she could feel people staring at her. I told her it didn't matter what anybody thought; that nothing could keep me from loving her. And if she didn't feel comfortable going to church she didn't have to go anymore.

The more I had sex with Pam, the more the preacher preached about sin, the more he preached about sin, the more I read in the Bible about relationships men had with God and how their willingness to forsake all-give up everything for Him-set them apart from the average man, and this granted them the miracle of the impossible being made possible.

For the first time in our seven months together I attempted the thought of being without Pam; and in the little space of that attempt was a vision of a world of unknown pain that I vowed never to see again. By opposing love there hate is created and I knew that the loser in this war of desire would have to become my enemy to secure my position with the winner. This night she wore light colored blue jeans-tight enough to punctuate the dividing of the lips of her vagina. Her beauty was the eighth wonder of the world, and I was immediately hypnotized by the sensual smell of her new perfume-a smell I never smelled again, but both desired and feared to smell again.

The past month had been filled with guilt after sex but this night her beauty controlled everything. Passion's heat brought the mist of sweat on my forehead-I was a lion ready to mate-but before I tore at her body I went to open the window to prepare our afterglow for the evening breeze. And as I opened the window I heard it, and felt it, a stern loud whisper saying,

"You have to chose between me and Pam."

I responded in my mind as quickly as I heard it,

"Please God, don't make me do that."

I told Pam I had to use the restroom so that she wouldn't see any change of heart in me and in the restroom I fell on my knees and my heart ached out to God,

"Whatever you have to do, take this girl away from

me."

In my mind I tried to believe that God could give me someone better, but my body's motion was still controlled by Pam. I zombied into the room, a baby in her arms, my clothes became chains, and before I could free myself, Pam grabbed my hands around the latch of my belt, and her words, "I can't do this anymore," spilled ice cold water on desire's fire that would have become my God for the rest of my life.

She was in God's hands! She said she felt guilty and didn't want to be the one responsible for keeping me from serving God and that one day, when I look back on this, I would thank her for it. I felt at that moment the Andre' she knew slip away and die into a memory as God took full control over my life. I've never thanked Pam for that day, I've never turned back, but I longed for her and my peace was that the miracle-working God of the Bible owed me one. I believed the stories in the Bible of his faithfulness to those who had suffered loss for Him. And God would never forget what I did for Him because the devastating falls I would take in the years to come would be cushioned with an omnipresent net that would always allow me to come through and walk away safely upon my feet.

The Road To Paradise

I was sixteen when my second life started. I came into the knowledge of God's love for me and lost the understanding of family and friends due to my change. I entered into a spiritual world where God became my teacher, and life became the instrument of His teachings. And even though my experiences separated me from people, they engulfed me in God, and I fell into His vastness. It was here that I understood that Godly hand that had always given me leverage, to lift me higher then was expected. Now that my hunger was focused on one meal I stuffed myself each day with the words of God. I began to imitate the actions of the Bible character Daniel, who would pray to God three times a day.

The new Andre´ was on fire for God. I would go downtown and find the busiest corner crowded with people and preach about Jesus. I preached about Jesus on every bus ride I took. I sang about Jesus on the assembly line at work, and I shared about Jesus to my dad, who was worried about my new change.

My father was the kind of man other men lied about being. When he spoke, his voice was thunder and his eyes struck like lighting-he towered over me, and wore a holy man's beard. I was afraid of him, and he used that to suppress my decisions and enforce his will. And I knew that I could never become my own man until I could stand for something he didn't believe in.

My father had never touched drugs until he was forty years old. But after that, for the next ten years, drugs would rob him of his manhood, strip him of his pride, and finally convince him he was no match for its power. He told me that when my sister gave him a check to cash for five hundred dollars, he was supposed to borrow half the money, but he lost it all on drugs, trying to make a profit. He said that was the last draw of drugs making him something he never was-less than a man! And focusing on a higher power he said a little prayer and God gave him the power to finally defeat his worst enemy.

I remember the talks we would have during the ending time of his battle; his voice balanced, trying to hold on to the man he once knew. He would ask questions addressed as statements, of whether I thought any less of him. I would convince him, with the words he taught me, that I admired him as being my father. I reminded him of my new faith in God, and that the ability to stand up for what I believed in, regardless of the consequences, was something I learned by how he lived.

My father was the one who told me that principles, character, and honor, are the clothes a man should always be caught wearing, and no great man has ever died without them. I always kept our conversations concentrated on the man I knew, instead of the man the drugs wanted me to see, because the mask the drugs had placed over my father's life made it impossible, in his present surroundings, to believe the man I spoke of ever existed.

My aunt Vanessa raised me from the time I was two until I was seven, but I was five when my dad visited me when I could first remember his years of bliss. We drove to his house in the Hollywood Hills. It had palace entry doors and multiple steps leading up to the dinning room. I took the passage through the kitchen, leading to the master bedroom that had a sliding glass door, that led me to the pool. I could feel the massive mountains surrounding the pool and the huge rocks that seemed to protect it. I played chase with lizards who would sometimes lose their tail in their struggle to get away. There was a fish tank with an Oscar in it that I was warned to keep my fingers out of, but when no one was looking, I put little rocks in there to see if he was mean as I was told. Michael Jackson's song "Rock With You," was playing and I'll never forget dancing to it with my dad. My two days there sealed my decision that one day I would be wherever he was.

Compassion is a gem found in the broken-hearted, and understanding is given through failure and tragedy. From the beginning of time there have been lives predestined by God for perfect trouble, and my life had been chosen for many appointments. Because my zeal for God came without wisdom, error was set for action, and the Divine discipline that followed my error, I learned, was the humbling tool God uses to make holy men. Time is an enemy to the afflicted, and patience is created by the stripping of haste that trouble demands. In the shadows that cover truth, that exists between losing and finding oneself, I found that seeking righteousness led me to self-examination. Looking close at the mirror's reflection of my life, is when I saw that my imperfection is what God used to spur the seeking in me to desire righteousness. Humiliation is associated with seeking righteousness-to expose the intents of the heart.

I remember a dream I had when I was eighteen. I was naked in front of everybody in the church I was going to, and I ran to the restroom for cover. I asked God in my dream why did he let all this happen to me. God said with a loud and strong voice that shock me awoke, "To Humble You." I knew then I was going to face a lot of hard and humiliating situations in the future, and that it was His will to allow me to face adversity so that He could mold my character, and shape my spirit to triumph.

It was Diana, my first wife, who was instrumental in one of my deaths traveling the road to paradise. From the beginning, the scale of reason was slanted. I was eighteen, she was thirty. Yet my experience gave me knowledge over her age, and her age was the wrong reason to like her. Days of laughter are remembered with a reassuring smile, and grief is a lasting stronghold that reminds you of past pains. I'll never forget the travailing pain of my relationship with Diana, and the stillborn marriage we gave birth to. She wasn't what I would normally look for in my choice of women, but everything I thought I needed to prove to myself that my love for God was stronger than my desire of what pleased me in a woman. Maybe it was her being pregnant that gave me the will to be selfless, or maybe it was the socialization of religion that it was the right thing to do. I believed my godly love could carry us without the flame of desire's passion. I thought that sacrificing what I wanted for the wants of another person was a righteous endeavor. But through this experience I understood the difference between being religious and being spiritual. Diana and I met in church almost a year into my new faith, I was radiant with confidence.

Diana, her sister, and brother-in-law gave their lives

to Jesus that day, and were there to here me share with the church the things I had learned during my first year there. It was my speaking that drew people to me, and the theatrical way I expressed my feelings made people like me even more. I was thirty in experience and seventeen in age, and my age would be the reason the church would close the curtain of their eyes, and the door of their ears in disbelief that I could understand my aged speaking. The other seventeen year olds that grew up in the church were not yet hardened and convinced by the knowledge one gains through experience. So when they spoke, it was what they thought was right from the convictions of an older person. How could they understand? I had lived a life from a child to sixteen exposed to pimps, prostitutes and drugs-a life their eyes only glimpsed passing by, or marveled at in a movie.

    The church never knew how to receive me, nor how to birth the gift within me. God chose me to be birthed outside of the box of religion, where man has imprisoned Him. The church has a lot of good people in it with a lot of bad ways. They nurture an act of good openly, while projecting righteousness that they tally within themselves. They harbor hidden deceit, and gorge on gossip, while forgetting that holiness is only achieved through the purging of the inner man.

Chapter Two: The Street Life

The street life is the material God used to cement me. There could have been no greater training camp, nor formidable opponent, to exercise and leverage my beliefs and promises against. On the streets, in the hustle, mistakes can cost you your life. The streets are callous, unrelenting...and they know who doesn't belong there. I was unfazed by the streets. Having been born from a prostitute and a pimp, nothing the streets could show me was new. I brought my new faith in God, who had communed and talked with me, so I felt empowered-ready for whatever.

So who would have ever thought I'd end up doing the thing I most despised, pimping? One thing is for certain; whatever I involved myself in I did with every bit of strength in me-with all my heart-because I believed if I didn't, I could never get through it. I already knew a lot about the pimp life and it was much different from how it was portrayed on TV, although those characters did exist. When I was a child growing up in that life I never saw a prostitute, I saw someone who loved, fed and disciplined me. My father wore business suits and quoted Shakespeare. It was only when I was older that I understood what I was seeing. I only grew to despise that life by what I thought was normal in my friend's lives. To me, it was fun treating all my friends on Fridays when I got my one hundred and fifty dollar allowance. It was fun being the kid with the money, until my dad got hooked on drugs. I know now that the destruction of my father's life, kept me away from drugs and alcohol and gave me the venom to hate it. Even when I became a pimp, I didn't allow the girls to drink alcohol or 'do' drugs, and the only time I wanted to get violent with them is when they would sneak off to do it.

The pimp life to me was like a family-a family of have-nots. The mindset of have-nots is much different from average people, and this actually gives them the ability to be freer in some instances. The average person grades or judges faithfulness or the lack of it, by sex in the relationship, but the people living in the subculture of the pimp life have learned to love beyond sex. What gives them validation and power is knowing they've conquered an emotion connected to sex that can destroy the average person and his or her relationship. I've learned deep truths about the workings of women and men that could have never been achieved outside of experiencing this lifestyle. In this subculture, the objective to succeed is greater then sex, so the passion of sex is tempered and prioritized. Satan has used sex to destroy everything, because it goes unchecked and because of people's fear, and lack of understanding. God sent me deep into the mud to find it, and make it bow, learn it at its worst, so I could control it. Do you think God wanted something he created as one of the pleasures between man and woman to be worshiped, held with such esteem that it can stop you, offset your objective, which is to "...press to the mark, for the prize, of the high calling of God"? It shouldn't even come close! The act of murder couldn't even stop Moses from fulfilling his God-given purpose.

The pimp life taught me how to be a king and govern over men and women with the truth. I know some of you are wondering how can that be. Well, for example, if the average man has a wife or girlfriend and he wants to get involved with another woman, he lies and becomes deceitful to do so. In the pimp life this action is looked down upon-so much so that if you did this, you wouldn't be considered a pimp. It is considered weak and unmanly to hide in the shadows and allow fear or attraction lessen and change who you say you are, just to get a woman. What a man should understand is that when a woman sees a man poised, unfazed and confident, he's an attraction already no matter what he does or looks like. That's why in the pimp life you may see some unattractive men with beautiful women. That life gave me above average restraint. For example, if I had a woman that had been with me for a day or ten years, and she left to be with another pimp, the act of a pimp would be to allow him to come and get her belongings, shake his hand and accept it. To act any way out of character by fighting, cursing, or threatening him would be the actions of a square, which would make him unfit to be in our subculture. What we understand is that it isn't the other pimp's fault she wanted to leave, and that acting a fool or crying won't make her come back. But at no time can you compromise the man, even if the cost is pain and great loss. This is what God wanted me to learn from that lifestyle; that even if my wife, whom I love, who's been married to me for seven years, chose to leave or be unfaithful, it wouldn't even break my stride!

I had a dream when I was around nineteen. In the dream I was walking down this road, until I came to the bottom of this rock-like mountain. I began to levitate to the top of the mountain and when I got to the top, it was level. Jesus was there and when I looked at Him, He was wearing cowboy boots with spurs. I began to walk with Him and He spoke to me, "Two kings shall rise up against you" and then I woke up. I never understood or knew what Jesus meant until years later, when the trouble came.

I remember sitting in my living room in my house of dreams. I said to myself, I did it, I made it to the top, and did all I could do in this life style. God must have agreed because not a week later the police came and kicked in the door, and it all came falling down. They said that I was living off of the earnings of prostitutes, and took me and two girls to jail-they let one go. I bailed everyone out the same day. A week later, when I was out of town, they came back saying that I had kidnaped the one girl they let go and that she was a juvenile. Hence came the first king, the state of Nevada. I knew I hadn't kidnaped anyone, but they put her in juvenile detention and tried to press her to lie on me. It took eight months of fighting before the truth came out and I was vindicated-but it wasn't over. The state of Nevada was so angry that their case didn't stick, because they had made a big deal about me and the way I was living, that they put me on the news like I was public enemy number one, and made me out to look like a real monster. Then they went to the Federal Government to ask them to assist in prosecuting me. So two months after I got out of jail I was indicted by the Feds. Hence came the second king. My case was the first time the state of Nevada and the Federal Government came together to prosecute a pimp case. This was very scary, and serious. I was facing life in prison for the alleged kidnaping, and even though I didn't do it, injustices have happened. I did know that this was a spiritual situation, and that the enemy was going to try to use this situation to destroy me by making me lose my faith. But the State of Nevada and the Government didn't know I had promises from God, and that I had seen them coming many years before they saw me.

The vice officer that was leading the case was obsessed with me. I think it was because when the police were in my house taking all my furniture, I told him, "you think I'm worried about this stuff? You can take all this stuff, but you can't take the mind that got it for me." God even gave me a dream about the vice officer when all this was going on. He said, "I chose him because he was a formidable opponent for you." This situation grew to become very consuming, and then I understood why God showed me about the two kings so many years in advance. Up to that point there was nothing I ever faced that even came close to the magnitude of this mountain of a problem. I knew that had it not been for all the visions, dreams, prophesies, manifestations and a proven track record that God was with me, this situation would have consumed me easily. I also understood at this point what the spurs on Jesus' boots symbolized; they symbolized that when this situation comes it would accelerate my life and spur me to another level. This was my lion's den, my burning fiery furnace, and my Goliath, and nothing in this world was going to make me lose my opportunity to stand tall. And it didn't matter if I was facing life in prison, or that the Feds and the State of Nevada joined to rise against me, or that other inmates who fought them got crushed. I was going to show them that there wasn't a pit deep enough that my God couldn't dig me out of.

Up to that point, I had been in God's training camp for thirteen years putting my life and freedom on the line for what I believed. Every situation that came to challenge what I believed in, I viewed with death: the women, the streets, the disappointments, pains, hurts, fears... anything that opposed my faith in God, was looked at with the willingness to die before I would let that happen. The streets finalized death in me, which made me unattached, and impenetrable by the world. God did move for me, even though they kept the girl in juvenile for eight months with the vice officers pressing her to lie.

When the preliminary hearing came, she got on the stand and told the court that everything I was accused of doing to her was a lie, and the first king and the life sentence came tumbling down. In the Federal trial, the

Government was seeking sixteen years. This king was much mightier He took the same girl and put her in front of the Federal Grand Jury and by threatening, scared her into a lie. I had already been in Federal custody for a year and when my three-day trial ended, I was found guilty on six charges. The newspaper reporters and my wife were there and they reported, "after the guilty verdicts were read, he looked over at his wife, and pointed upwards, and said 'no matter what, believe in Him!" My charges were multiple counts of the Mann Act, which is transporting a person across state lines for immoral purposes, and money laundering.

At the sentencing, God showed up again. The judge said that he couldn't sentence me because he had a problem with three of the six verdicts and he wanted my attorney to make a motion so he could dismiss them. Now understand this, it was after I was found guilty of the charges that the judge wanted to dismiss them. So when I came back for sentencing a couple of months later, I was only sentenced on three charges, and the most severe charge was money laundering. I received 65 months and the judge did something else that wasn't common-he gave me 20 months off of my Federal sentence for the time I spent fighting my case in the state. He gave me eight months for the time I was in state custody, and made my time run concurrent with the 12 months I was in Federal custody. I ended up with 45 months and was credited with another 12 months in custody that it took for me to fight the case. When I was fighting my state case the Feds came to me to make a deal, it was called a pre-indictment deal. They offered me five years, that would include the state case and their case, if they decided to indict me. Everyone knows that if you take the Feds to trial and lose, they're going to stick it to you. But because I believed God, and because of all the things I had experienced walking with Him, He moved for me and I ended up with less time than the deal they offered. I remember before the judge sentenced me, he asked me if I had something to say. I said, "Yes I was born from the womb of a prostitute and by the seed of a pimp. At least that's what society says, but in actuality they were my mother and father. And the people you consider the scum of the earth were the people who hugged me, fed me, and caressed me. And even if you wanted me to, I couldn't think of them the way you do, and I don't think this lifestyle is a criminal act. I think that it's immoral before God but man shouldn't be the one that judges it." And with that the courtroom fell silent, and without the judge saying so, God let him know that I had purpose in my life.

One night, in my jail cell, I was reflecting and I couldn't understand why God would go so far out of His way, it seemed, to make me know beyond any doubt that He was with me and in control, even in the muddiest places of my life. Well, that night I had a dream; there was a man who was a murderer, and not just any murderer, he would kill children and families. He would find a high-rise building and place their body parts in some type of devil worship position, real big so that the media could televise it and show it to the world. Now because he killed children and families in the fashion he did, he was the most hated man upon the face of the earth. But in the dream, God let me feel his love for the man and I was in awe, because the love God had for the man was so beautiful that it was hard for me to understand. The whole world was looking for this man. The police got a tip on where he was, and the chase began. He led them on a chase in a car, and when he got a little distance, he got out by some apartments and started running. He ran through the building looking for open doors. In the dream my heart was racing because one of doors he tried to open was unlocked and I knew there was a family inside. He went in and there were two little girls, an older boy, and the mother and father. I felt like he was going to kill them. The police knew he ran through the apartments and were going door-to-door, until they came to the family's door. When they went in, no one was hurt, and the man just game himself up; the police handcuffed him and brought him out. I could feel the hatred in one of the police officer's heart, and I knew he wanted to kill the man. So as they were walking upstairs to get to the main level, the police officer pushed the man and made him stumble.

On the main level there were hundreds of policemen with their guns drawn, so when the man stumbled the police officer who pushed him yelled, "he's trying to get away," and shot him. The other police officers began to shoot also, but in the dream, God was angry at the officer because he wanted the man to have a fair trial. So God stepped in and didn't allow any of those bullets to harm the man, and everyone was in awe and knew that God had saved him. The police, media, and the world saw the miracle before their eyes, and when the man saw that he was saved by God, his heart changed and became beautiful. He was set free, because of the miracle, and began to tell his story all over the world. He went on the Oprah Winfrey show, and shared everywhere what God had done for him, and the world loved him. And God spoke to me in the dream and said, "If I loved him, the most hated man in the whole world, how much more do you think I love you?" I awoke in tears engulfed in His love.

Chapter Three: Athena

In my sleep God spoke to me! "You're going to get married again, and your wife is going to be just like you."

When I found my wife Athena, I realized that treasures are hidden in dark and deep places to discourage the pursuit of average men. There have been amateur explorers that have stumbled across her whereabouts, but their vision shot of light made it impossible for them to dig beyond the efforts of those who failed. At first sight her green eyes unfairly took me at a disadvantage. She was evenly uneven with every woman of my past, and she was my accumulation of knowledge of what I knew to look for in my ideal woman. She was the sweet that took away the taste of my every bitter relationship, and my heart welcomed her, free from the fear of disappointment harnessed by the tainted unknown. She grew into me like a child grows into their adult teeth, and knowing it was her time to come, I could feel her underneath my skin waiting for the passing of my old life.

True love is a seed of appreciation that grows from understanding what one has from the failure of past relationships. I met Athena in 1998 when I was on the run from the police. I was in San Diego for the Superbowl, looking to make some money because of my troubles in

Las Vegas. It was the Saturday before Superbowl Sunday and I was at the hotel thinking about everything that had happened. I decided to go to a club to keep things off of my mind. It was the Blue Tattoo, the club where I first saw Athena and approached her. We exchanged names and looks, and finally got on the dance floor. While we were dancing, the music magic became a magnet that drew our metal hearts together, and liquefied them into one dance that became an equally matched exploit of problems being released from a troubled soul.

We didn't see each other again until after a week of laughing and sharing on the phone. She was very receptive when I spoke to her about God and how you can never put Him in a box. But that if you want something from God badly enough, you can have it, if you're willing to give up your life to believe Him for it. I felt so comfortable with her, and so weighed down by my life-she was so new, and I would have never seen her in that light, separate from the life I led, had the end of my yesterday never happened.

I remember the first time entering the twin doors of her tunnel's rigid opening and feeling heat when her hallways released the lube that guided my movement like a tractor beam. There was a language in her hands when she touched me, and the way that her eyes saw was strong-not just physically, but something came alive deep inside of her that I could feel almost died waiting for the opportunity to prove itself. I knew, eventually, I would have to tell her about my life and that seemed so distant from the place that I was at with her. I believe it was God's will that I was stripped of everything before I met her because He wanted me to see the actions of purity uncontaminated by money.

I had already disfranchised myself as a pimp when I crossed the barrier and saw her as my own. I told her everything about me, from my mother and father, to Pam, to meeting God and all the things He showed and told me about my future. I told her all the things I had faced and conquered and finally, how I became a pimp. I was at the end of that life and I didn't even desire it anymore, but I knew she had come into my life for a reason. I told her what had happened in Las Vegas, and that eventually I would go to prison, but that I didn't care because I knew my God would be there for me. Athena looked into me and said, "and I am to!" I believed her when she said it. We only had two months together, but we fell in love. When the police did catch up with me, I was weary of running and ready to face my accusers.

It happened in March of 1998, when Athena and I were in Los Angeles so she could meet my father. We were staying at a hotel I had stayed at many times before. The police in Vegas looked through my paperwork and found credit card statements of places I'd stayed. They sent pictures to those places and told them that if I showed up, to call the local authorities. They had the maintenance man knock on my door and identify himself, and when I opened the door, the marshals and police arrested me and I was expedited back to Las Vegas, and Athena went back home to San Diego.

We talked on the phone for a full month and ran up a seven thousand dollar phone bill, and it wasn't disconnected until after she moved from San Diego, leaving family, friends, and security, to be by my side to support me in jail. I remember asking my wife, in one of our phone conversations, if she believed physical love was stronger than spiritual love. I told her that I have never seen God the way I see her, and that I never hugged God the way I've hugged her, but that my love for God is unmatched by any other. I told her that the love we share would have to be centered within God's deeper love, and that there would be nothing that could overwhelm us in the strength of this love, regardless of what the courts, the newspapers, or people say, and that if we believe and continue within this love, we will overcome everything.

Every visiting day of every month, Athena was there, and I never saw a worry in her eyes. It had been seven months of us looking through Plexiglas before we decided it wouldn't stop us from being together before God as one.

We were married on the third of October, nineteen hundred and ninety-eight, a month before the victory over the first king. In state custody God had given me a dream that when I got out, I would be indicted by the Federal Government. I told Athena this, and everything she saw come to pass, gave her resolve, and cemented her faith that God was in control.

After being released from state custody, I had a dream before my indictment. In the dream, the police were chasing me and two women. I told the women that if they followed me real close, they would get away. They followed me a little way, but then fell off. I was climbing over fences, running over bridges, and doing some miraculous things to get away. Then towards the end I saw Athena get behind me and start following me; everything I did, she did step for step. We ended up going to the top floor of this apartment. In the apartment, there were clothes lying everywhere. We begin to change clothes; the police were thinking they should knock down the front door, and there were other police officers of high rank trying to get in through the window. I took an ink pen and sprayed the police by the window and they fell off. I noticed that a crowd had gathered in the streets-police, friends, strangers, and some family. I could feel them wondering what I was going to do next, so I went on the balcony looking for a way of escape. I thought about jumping to the next building or to the balcony below me. While I was wondering what to do, God spoke to me in the dream and said, "Andre you don't have to run anymore, jump into the crowd." I came inside and told Athena what God had said, and she was ready, so we went on the balcony and jumped into the crowd. And God showed me that before we would hit the bottom, He would move and cause us to disappear right before everyone's eyes. I awoke and told Athena the dream and my interpretation of it.

The two women represented women that had been with me that didn't have enough faith to make it all the way. Crossing the fences and the bridges represented the different levels I've been able to get to with God's miraculous help. And you coming towards the end following me step by step is now. The apartment with clothes everywhere, represents a transitional place that I'd come to many times before. The changing of the clothes represented the new walk of life we will have. The police at the door were the state police who first started the pursuit, and the high ranking police trying to get in through the window were the Feds. The ink that I sprayed to make them fall was God showing us that it will be paperwork that will defeat the Feds. The crowd is everyone who was following the case. God telling me I, "don't have to run anymore, jump into the crowd," is closure and God telling me to go to trial and face my opposition. And when everyone thinks it's the end for us, God would supernaturally move on our behalf for everyone to see.

One thing Athena never lacked was faith. She was always quick to believe and act, even if things looked bleak. When she moved from San Diego, she rented a U-haul, packed her belongings, and left on faith to Las Vegas without a place to live, only a destination. In Las Vegas she got a weekly motel, in hopes on being able to find a job before she spent the last of her money on the next week. The U-haul was due back a couple of days after she got there, and keeping it longer than its due date cost her more than the few hundred dollars.

One morning she got up and the U-haul wasn't there- all of her clothes and furniture taken with it. She called the U-haul place and they said they wouldn't release anything until the late fees were paid. They ended up auctioning off all of her belongings, and wouldn't even give her back anything sentimental. The plan was for her to come to Vegas, get a job, put the furniture in storage, and find a place. But none of that worked out. The eight months Athena was in Las Vegas to be my support, she moved from motel to motel, lost all of her belongings, but never once missed a visiting day to see my face and smile. In all that time she never had a car, it was on the bus that she came to see me, even when the day went dark.

I was in Federal custody when Athena got her job and a place, and she supported me the entire year it took to go to trial. After I was found guilty and sentenced, the Feds shipped me to Tucson, Arizona. Athena packed up everything again and, thank God because she was able to transfer her job to an office they had in Phoenix, Arizona an hour outside of Tucson. Athena got a place the day she arrived, and was able to visit me within the week. What made this visit a special event, was that for the 14 months in Federal custody I hadn't embraced her or even touched her; I had only seen her through emotionless glass. Now, after 14 months of battling, our unwavering hearts touched again.

The next move the Government made trying the boundaries of love, was sending me to Victorville,

California to fill up their new prison. Athena was undaunted. After six months of being in Arizona, it was time to follow me to California. She was able to stay with my father, in which a beautiful relationship was built. A friend of mine, Gene, who offered friendship and finances throughout my incarceration, gave her thirty five hundred dollars to buy a car so she could take the two hour drive and visit me in Victorville. It was eight months after being in the Victorville prison that the world witnessed fate, faith and love overcome all obstacles, when I was released to the promise, and joy, of the wife who would be just like me.

Chapter Four: The Knowledge

The Road To Paradise

In My sleep God Spoke To Me: "I'll be the only one on your right hand; everyone else will be on your left."

The Road to Paradise is laden with mirrors of self examination, and faith is essential to help one overcome the disheartening things you're going to see and face. Faith that has been tried, faith that has been proven, and faith that has worked before, is faith qualified to give your life for. Faith is a lifestyle, and its intent is to fly its' carrier to the supernatural realm of God uninterrupted by human fear, emotion and high above circumstances and situations. *"Through faith we understand that the worlds were framed by the words of God, so that things which are seen were not made of things which do appear."*(Hebrews 11:3) Now listen very closely and let me tell you how miracles happen. God is bound by His own Word. This means that God and His Word are one and the only thing God can't do is lie or change. *"For I am the Lord, I change not."*(Malachi 3:6). God's Word is life unchanging, unaffected by nature, and complete with all existence submitted to it. Everything created is imperfect because of its ability to change. The definition of evolution is, "A gradual process in which something changes into a different or more complex form." But perfection can only be attained by aligning yourself with truths that never change. Therefore, the evidence of God's existence is having the ability to create supernatural happenings through having faith in words that never change. When you align yourself with perfection, you're in the realm of the supernatural were miracles live.

There are two worlds: the spiritual and the natural world. If you could see into the spiritual world, you would see God's word like a golden rope, stretched perfectly from the beginning of time in the earth, to the end of time in heaven. And on that rope you would see time lines that determine events, devastations, the rise and fall of kingdoms and the end of time. You would even be able to see what your life consisted of, what your purpose was and what God planned for you. But only *faith* can get you into this unseen world.

The natural world consist of what you see daily-the power of man, the oppression of circumstances, and the fear of the unknown. Every man is a servant to what he believes in, so the man that doesn't believe in the existence of God is subject to man's power, oppression and circumstances. But faith in God activates supernatural power and aligns your life with the working of miracles, so that the elements of the natural world that would confine you are without effect. This power that elevates

The Road To Paradise

you above natural elements and human conditions is not your own. You've tapped into its resources by faith. *"This is the word of the Lord saying not by might, not by power, but by my spirit saith the Lord."(Zechariah 4:6)* Once you've aligned yourself with the eternal purpose of existence which is God's Word fulfilling itself, your every step becomes ordered by God; every circumstance and situation that comes must first be sanctioned and allowed by God. People often wonder why God doesn't just make Himself known. He tried that before and men loved the things of this world more than Him. So He decided that He would hide His physical existence until the ones that longed for Him more than the things of this world, would, through their efforts of faith, try to reach Him.

Faith is the compass to God and when reached the walk begins, now you've become a part of them who know some of the secrets of God's plan. He starts by letting you see parts of your future, and some of the worlds future. Faith allows you to see God's plan before the natural world materializes it, which gives the holder of faith an advantage. "For God will surely do nothing, except He first reveal it to his servants the prophets." If you are in a contrary situation, no matter how impossible it looks, because of faith you can be unaffected, high above the circumstances and situation of the natural world, knowing that the elements of this world must align themselves to fulfill God's Word.

In the natural realm, problems are isolated. In the spiritual world, everything happens as a whole, as a part of a complete purpose, since the beginning of time. *"I have esteemed the words of His mouth more than my necessary food."* (Job 23:12) The Book of Job is believed to be the oldest of sacred writings. In this story of real life past events, we understand that Job is a perfect and upright man. He has vast wealth, a beautiful family, and God allows his faith to be tested. But before I share some spiritual insight about this situation, let me first qualify your understanding. First, faith is a seed that is watered and perfected by opposition; the more opposition it faces and conquers, the more perfect it becomes. You would have to spend many years advancing through many levels of faith for God to allow the Job syndrome to come upon your life. Job was a blessed man in his natural life, and especially in his spiritual life; God called him perfect. Now when God calls you perfect, this qualifies you for events and circumstances so contrary, devastating, and consuming that only the man of perfected faith can stand through it. Job's perfected faith was the ultimate compliment to God, so God wagered on Job's faith, so that He could use

Job's life as an example of the strength of faith, against man's greatest feelings of emotion and affection. God allowed Job to be stripped of all his wealth, then allowed his ten children to be killed. He was afflicted with boils over his entire body, and finally his own wife lost faith in him. *"He that loveth father or mother, son or daughter more than me is not worthy of me" (Matthew 10:3)* Would you fare well if your faith was called upon to prove its loyalty and steadfastness, despite the tragedy of great loss?

Defiance is one of the attributes of perfected faith; sacrifice is another. The man of faith is willing to stand up in defiance against any obstacle and element that opposes what he believes in. No matter how improbable the win looks in the natural realm, he is willing to sacrifice his most sacred trust-his life. This makes everything else around him expendable when it opposes faith in God's word. Job lost everything but faith. He didn't understand why all this bad had happened to him, but faith is not based on your understanding. Job's body was full of boils and his heart and feelings were crushed to the lowest despair. But faith is not based upon your physical strength, nor on how you feel. Job had no knowledge of the cause of his misfortune, but he knew that God was in control of his life, and had to have allowed this to happen. Job was fixed on faith because he knew faith was the only measurement of perfectness and righteousness, in this confusing storm that had now consumed and destroyed his life. And this is why Job said, *"My foot hath held His steps, His way have I kept, and not declined. Neither have I gone back from the commandments of His lips, I have esteemed the words of His mouth more than my necessary food."(Job 23:11-12)* Job knew that one word from God could bring order to a whole generation in chaos, he knew that faith was the key to Devine order in life, and no matter what he valued, or who he loved in this world, nothing would even come close to his value of his faith in God.

King David was another biblical figure who used faith to triumph over his monstrous physical enemies. Everyone has heard about the story of David and Goliath and there are many general meanings to the story. But we will go inside to its core and pull out the substance of its truth. David's father had put him in charge of the family's sheep because his older brothers where in the army. He was about sixteen years old and one day he was called in by his father from watching the sheep. And there stood the holy prophet Samuel, waiting for him with anxious eyes. Samuel said to David, "One day you will be king over Israel," and with that word of promise Samuel anointed

The Road To Paradise

David king. From that day forward, David knew his life was connected to the perfect, unchanging, power of God's Word.

David went back to keeping the sheep, until one day his father told him to go and check on his brothers in the army. When David got there he saw and heard something that made him defiant. *"Goliath a giant that stood around ten feet tall, with massive body armor, a large terrifying spear, challenge the armies of Israel, to send a man that would fight him."(1 Samuel 17:4-8)* But all of the men in Israel's army were afraid. However David heard the challenge, and wanted to fight this giant. The acting king at that time couldn't see how a boy such as David could have so much courage and poise when everyone else was afraid. *"And Saul said to David, thou art not able to go against this Philistine to fight him, for thou art but a youth, and he a man of war from his youth."(1 Samuel 17:3)* The kings response to David is the reason why a man without faith can't please God, because he allows what he sees in front of him to cause him fear, and not to act. For faith to work you must *act* upon it. The man without faith relies on reason, muscle, or intellect to decide his battles, so David began to explain why he was so courageous.

He told the king that he's in charge of the family's sheep, and that there was a time that a lion came and grabbed one of them. He went after it and took the sheep out of the lion's mouth, and when the lion turned to attack him, he killed it with his bare hands. He said the same thing happened with a bear, and the same God that delivered him out of the paw of the lion and the bear, will deliver him out of the hands of Goliath, the Philistine. One thing is for sure, when you start out conquering Goliaths, God won't put you in battles of faith that he has not equipped you for. This goes back to what I wrote in the beginning of the chapter-faith that has been tried, faith that has been proven, and faith that has worked before, is faith qualified to give your life for. David understood this, because David had history with God. His faith had grown to such a level that he was willing to give up his life to trust it, and that's the very thing that makes it work, the very thing that makes the miracle happen. David knew that God had delivered him from the lion and the bear, he experienced that for himself, that was his own personal anchor, his own personal manifestation of Gods realness, and the power that comes by faith in Him. Always remember, you just don't start out conquering Goliaths, you have to first face, and conquer the lion and the bear in your life.

I want you to notice the two different equipments of power. First, Goliath by nature was an above average man, he no doubt possessed the strength of two or three men. He had the most advanced weapons of war and defensive body armor of his day. From a child he was trained for killing, "and a man of war from his youth." He was far superior in every area than any warrior in Israel's army, and so much so, he terrified them. Goliath is the complete package of what man and nature has to offer as their winner, but David had one thing from the start that made the gift that nature gave to Goliath less than nothing. David had a word from God that one day he would be king. And one promise from God destroys whatever opposition that man or nature sets forward. That one promise God gave David would have been enough, but faith has a way of over qualifying its inheritor, to make you *"more than a conquer."(Romans 8:37)* God allowed the word he gave to David to be tested and tried through opposition, so he would know and be overly sure, that God was with him. God knows that the experience of your faith being tried is much *"more precious than gold."*(1 Peter 1:7) It also adds Godly character and poise, which are necessary for a king. David was overly ready for the task that the men without faith feared. This shows that there are certain situations that come about in life that require faith to stand in, because the man without faith will crumble, do to what he accumulates in his mind, and what he sees with his natural eyes, as terror. There are many forms of Goliaths: adverse circumstances, corrupt governments, oppression, natural elements, and disease. All these things are subject to faith in God's word. Most people live in a world where circumstances and situations shape their lives. They feel you have to accept what you get and do the best you can with it, and the more influential people they know, the better off their lives will be. They desire to connect themselves with conglomerate forces, government, corporations, and banks. People seek protection and favor and want to become, or be affiliated with, Goliath because that's how the natural mind works. People without faith, have made man's power their God, because they have seen the evidence of man's power in the world. This is why God used David, who was a sheepherder, because most people who are born advantaged feel they have no need of faith since the world is already at their disposal. That attitude is why God mostly uses disadvantaged people to prove a point and frustrate and humble the powers of man. "*The foolishness of God is wiser than man, and the weakness of God is stronger than man. For you see your calling brethren, how* that not many wise men after the flesh, not many mighty, not many noble, are called. But God has chosen the foolish things of this world to confound the wise, and God has chosen the weak things of this world to confound the things which are mighty. And base things of the world, and things which are despised, hath God chosen."(1 Corinthians 1:25-28)

Thus saith the Lord "I have chosen the drunk, the drug addict, and the mentally insane because they hear me."

The new Holy men and women of today will be defiant, with the proof of power from heaven on their side, and they will have been well hidden, adequately prepared for the lack of faith and the advancement of technology this age prides itself in. They will be violent in their convictions and exploits of faith, and will run into battle against faiths opposition. They will be willing to sacrifice their lives as a token of their love for their God, and they will prepare the way for the coming of the Lord.

In my sleep god spoke to me: "You will stand before my people and tell them where I brought you from"

A man is never afraid to make a decision, even if he must stand alone to do so. He's not intimidated by past failures and never allows them to block his vision. He uses these past failures as a stepping stone, because he knows that a decision made, even if it's wrong, gives him experience, and experience gives knowledge, and knowledge produces growth. And while men who are undeveloped are immobilized by wallowing in past failures, the man of God arrays himself in faith, ready to conquer any mountain that comes his way. He views the world through the eyes of God and rises out of darkness, out of negativity, and out of failure, to become a giant in a world of undeveloped men.

There is great joy in teaching life's lessons, but development comes through experiencing them. You should charge after life, pursue it, examine it, taste it, touch it, and feel its wanting areas so that you can respect its conclusions. Because truth, wisdom, and understanding, are learned from error, tragedy, and mistakes. God has always used man's failure as a means of manifesting Himself, because failure is an end of pride, power, motivation, and it symbolizes death.

Thus saith the Lord "My desire is that men would be broken before me as tho they were dead."

Enlightenment and truth from God comes with a price tag that hangs between the balance of sacrifice and death. In the beginning pursuit of enlightenment, it will

The Road To Paradise

run and make you follow it to great depths, it will fly from you to mountain heights, and if the desire in you is a fire that will not be quenched by the flood waters of failure, you will find it, and it will reward you with truth and hidden wisdom. Life is the witness to who you really are; it has endless doors of self-discovery and reruns to stay in your memory. ~~Dying to self is the universal way to spirituality and purity~~, and while going through life's discoveries seeking truth, life's mirror will reflect and expose to you the ugly, evil, and filth of your true ways. You must first meet yourself before you can die to self. *"To nobody, O Illustrious One, can you communicate in words and teachings what happened to you in the hour of your enlightenment."*(Herman Hesse, Sidhartha)

Jesus wanted us to understand the necessity to engage life, and endure its heartbreaks. God places the mantle of discovery upon youth, and that's why he mixed strength with youth. *"Seeing then that we have a great high priest, that passed into the heavens, Jesus the Son of God, for we have not a high priest which cannot be touched with the feeling of our infirmities, but was in all points tempted like as we are, yet without sin."*(Hebrews 4:14-15) Youthfulness values and desires many vanities, and life entreats and entices it to desire and hold dear, because sacrificing is only felt with things you value. At the end of the road of discovering self, you'll find that uncontrolled lust, addiction to greed, compulsion to sexual adventure and striving for recognition and power, have only led you to the simple things in life. *"Remember now thy creator in the days of thy youth, while the evil days come not, nor the years draw nigh, when thou shalt say, I have no pleasure in them."(Ecclesiastes 12:1)*

The story of the prodigal son is a story of a young man's lust for the sensual pleasures of this world, and his journey through life's discoveries. The young man lived with his rich father and other brother, he had come of age and he burned with anticipation of experiencing life to its fullest, so his father gave him his inheritance and allowed him to leave. *"And not many days after the younger son gathered all together and took his journey into a far country, and there wasted his substance with riotous living."(Luke 15:13)* One must understand when a child comes of age they are entitled to make their own decisions and learn from their own mistakes. Life, the universal teacher, is the maze through which we find ourselves. His father understood this and had confidence in the foundation and base from which he raised his son. *"Train up a child in the way he should go, and when he is old, he will not depart from it."(Proverbs 22:6)* His father knew that he had done his part as a parent, and felt confident that the principles he taught his son would stand up and prevail against the delusions of life. Principles, Honor, and Integrity, hold the substance by which we should grade one another, and wherever life ends you, if these remain, you are close to heaven. Righteousness taught in youth is a compass to the soul to guide you through life's entanglements of right and wrong. The prodigal son would have to measure his choices of interest against who he was, and what had been instilled in him. He had wasted all his money on his heart's desire and then found himself in want, in a far away country. He had to get a job feeding swine and was so hungry he began to eat the swine's food, because no one would feed or help him. These are some of life's lessons which are necessary for the cultivation of character and revelation, to bring one to the truth within himself. The prodigal son's upbringing was his anchor and he was able to draw from the truth of his father's teachings to balance himself. He knew he'd gotten himself in some trouble due to his lust for worldly living, but he had come to himself by being brought to his end. His decision to pursue his lust had caused him failure, and failure caused him to examine his situation, the road he took, and his primary intent. Once failure is present one is either conquered by it or renewed by it. Failure is the opponent one must consistently conquer to become enlightened, and the spiritual principle for the development of character is "before honor is humility." Thus God used the prodigal son's failure as a refiner and buffer, to bring the truth to light, so that it may set him free from his error. Once he discovered his error and his eyes were opened, he thought about home, the love of his father, and the servants in his father's house that now lived better than him. He knew he had made a great mistake, and the chastisement of his error caused great shame. But the purity of his father's teaching began to sink in, and the value of righteous and holy living began to sink in until the shame consumed him so totally, he felt unworthy to be called his father's son. *"I will arise and go to my father, and will say unto him, father, I have sinned against heaven, and before you, and am no more worthy to be called thy son: make me as one of thy hired servants."*(Luke 15:18-19)

You must understand that God wants to bring you to repentance, and He will allow error in your ways, and mistakes in your judgement, to get you there. There are some who have judged those who have traveled through the worldly avenues of life, not knowing that God was building a leader. The prodigal sons brokenness, was God building a leader, his humiliation was God building a leader, and his desire to go back to where he started, was

The Road To Paradise

God building a leader. God doesn't choose His leaders by mans measurements; man wants a perfect man, who appears to have made no mistakes, a man whose past hasn't been tarnished with sinful living, and whose hands haven't been tainted by lust. But God chooses the man who has been knocked off the path of righteousness into the gutters of life, to deal with failure and adversity, to face his demons, and to know his nothingness. And when emptied of all the things men glory in, God begins to fill this man with the things that make a god. This is how cursings are turned into blessings, and this is how God defeats the results of sin. Nothingness is the foundation from which holy men are built. In despair, at one's lowest point of failure, error, and sin, you are closest to the heart of God, because you know what it is to be rejected by man. The prodigal son knew he had to get back to his father's house, where he remembered the beauty of holy living. He was even willing to be a servant, if that's what it took, because he now understood the value of truth and purity, and was willing to sacrifice anything to live within it again. His father forgave him because he learned the value of righteousness, and once you come to the place where you're willing to sacrifice position, reputation, and livelihood, for righteousness and truth, you have become enlightened.

André Taylor

> *In my sleep God spoke to me: "I'm God and I'm not dead, give this message to your family, there's not one prayer that you pray that goes by unheard."*

This was written in 1999.

Prayer is the cleansing place for the guilty, it is the guarded door of your faults, and the cry of the oppressed. There are many types of prayers, and all prayers are categorized according to its history and intent. Most prayers are not answered because they have no history surrounding them, they're alien, and may never reach the presence of God. But the prayer above all prayers is the prayer of forgiveness and cleansing. When people are in trouble they offer the prayer of help with no history connected to it, and that's why most of those prayers go unanswered. God values the prayer of forgiveness and cleansing far more than any trouble you're in, and more serious than whatever devastation has taken place. "*If my people, which are called by my name shall humble themselves and pray, and seek my face and turn from their wicked ways, then will I hear from heaven, and will forgive their sin, and will heal their land.*"(2 Chronicles 7:14) Prayers with history reveals years of a sacred meeting place, the struggles of life, and

The Road To Paradise

the confidence of faith. Panic and need initiates prayer, but its beginning should be submission of pride and the acknowledgment of sin. The lifeline of spirituality is prayer-the link that connects you to knowing God. Prayer is to release your fears, explain your hurts, and drain your tears, but it's not a means to bargain with God. Remember acknowledgment of sin and confession is the beginning of your prayers being answered, and God will respond to you if you persist in the ways of righteousness. How many times have you uttered a little prayer to God, in hopes that that's all it's going to take to get an answer? You offered nothing, you put in nothing, and you will get back nothing. God honors and smiles upon prayers that have endured time, reproach, and adversity.

There was a woman by the name of Hannah, who was one of two wives; the other woman had many children and Hannah had none. Year after year Hannah would pray and weep to God for a child, but no child would come. And year after year the other woman would gloat in this and try to provoke her, so that she would begin to hate God. The element of this situation is one of the primary reasons people turn their backs on God, and believe He doesn't exist. People feel that when they are suffering, that it is cause enough for God to hear their prayer, and when they pray and nothing changes, they become embittered and they begin to hate God. They reason that there can't be a God, that's so loving and caring, who can look down upon so much grief and pain, and not be moved to help. You cannot make God what you think he should be. God is not moved by one who reverences Him only when in need, or requiring rescue. Hannah understood this, and she wanted God to know that whether he answered her or not, she would continue to seek Him. Despite her disappointment, she would continue to pray. This is the kind of prayer that God answers, a prayer with history, that God can look over and remember. *"And they rose up in the morning early, and worshiped before the Lord, and returned and came to their house in Ramah, and Hanna and her husband made love, and the Lord remembered her."*(1 Samuel 1:19) Once Hannah got to the place where God was bigger than what she asked for, God answered her prayer. There's a place in God where one's life is not motivated by the things you want, but by the things you're willing to sacrifice, and when you reach that level you shall have everything you ask for. *"And she was in bitterness of soul, and prayed unto the Lord, and wept sore. And she vowed a vow, and said O'Lord of host, if thou would indeed look on the affliction of thine handmaid, and remember me, and not forget thine handmaid, but wilt give unto thine handmaid a man child, then I will give him unto the Lord all the days of his life." (1 Samuel 1:10-11)* God was waiting for Hannah to get to where she could live without what she prayed for, because what she wanted could not be loved more than Him. *"For where your treasure is, there will your heart be also." (Luke 12:34)* In God, things are done in perfect order, and one's faithfulness to Him is first priority. When you are consumed in pleasing God, the things you pray for are very easy to come by. When Hannah was willing to sacrifice the raising of her son, she knew her part would be minimal in his life, but Hannah had come to the place where she was willing to give up whatever God gave her at anytime. She wasn't moved by the situation anymore, she submitted her emotions to God's will, and rested in the peace that He was in control. God had a blessing for Hannah, but she couldn't receive the blessing until her priorities were in order. And the moment they were, God remembered Hannah, and blessed her to birth Samuel, one of the greatest prophets that ever lived. There is a reason behind every unanswered prayer, and to receive revelation of the reason, you must have patience and steadfastness, because the obstacle course your prayer will face is the proving ground of your desire.

Chapter Five: God's Demand for Payment

In my sleep God spoke to me: "This is a time for black people, the world is calling for black people."

Every Black person born in America in these times is a blessed seed, no matter what your condition is, homeless, poor, uneducated, or orphaned, you are the blessed seed. *"There are men who have suffered and who have not only gone on living, but even built a new fortune on the ruins of their former happiness. From the depths into which their enemies have plunged them, they have risen again with such vigor and glory, that they have dominated their former conquerors and cast them down in their turn."(Alexander Dumas, 'The Count of Monte Cristo')* Black people's prayers have endured four hundred years of the greatest atrocity known to man, slavery! Within these four hundred years are stories sadder than the word sad could explain, evil that words had no words for, and the abandoned prayers of many generations. Prayers that endured Black Men being dismembered and castrated, beaten and murdered for generations with no answer. Prayers that endured Black Women being raped and sodomized, from a child of ten, eleven, and twelve into adulthood, for generations, with no answer. Year after year, generation after generation, Black people prayed and there was no answer. These Black people died not seeing their prayers answered, died for a feeling they would never feel, yet bore on their backs the life of an animal, while praying for you to be free. Whatever you think you're going through today is nothing. I'm offended if you can look in the face of four hundred years of prayers that endured hardship, brokenness, and injustice you couldn't even fathom going through, and say to our ancestors that the price they paid for just our freedom alone, is not enough for you. They gave their lives to be a bum on the street, if that's what they wanted to do, to be a nobody if that's what they wanted to do, to just have the freedom to do whatever was their prayer. So the reason why the state of Black America is without direction, is because we refuse to remember where we came from so we can honor where we're at today.

The foundation of pain and struggle that binds us together as a people, that meeting place of remembering that keeps us grounded, that commitment of selflessness that furthers a people, is the prayers of our ancestors and the freedom they paid for us to have. And they're demanding to be remembered and honored. It is impossible for any people to go through so many atrocities, and pray that long and God not answer. So when we see Denzel Washington, Halle Berry, and Jamie Fox win the Academy Award, know that it's bigger than them, that

The Road To Paradise

it's the prayers of our ancestors, and God's demand for payment. When you see Michael Jordan fly, Kobe Bryant glide, and Shaq O'Neal dominate, and you marvel-know that it's bigger than them, that it's the prayers of our ancestors and God's demand for payment. When you see Oprah Winfrey and Robert Johnson become billionaires, and see rappers come from the gutters of life and build empires, know that it's bigger than them, that it's the prayers of our ancestors, and God's demand for payment. So Black Man, Woman, and Child, look at yourself again and see the blessed seed that you are, and know that your ancestors have already paid for you, and you were born walking in that blessing. So Black entertainers, sport stars, corporate leaders, and politicians, receive your accolades on behalf of your ancestors, the slaves that prayed you through.

In my sleep God spoke to me: "I have sprinkled you in my salt, but I will surly bring you out, for everyone must be sprinkled in my salt."

Salt is required before sacrifice, and sacrifice was the means of offering something precious to God for remission of sin, for peace, and for trespassing against someone. In the Levitical law, God demanded that the meat be seasoned with salt, before it's sacrificed, or it wouldn't be acceptable to him. "And every oblation of thy meat offering shalt thou season with salt, neither shalt thou suffer the salt of the covenant of thy God to be lacking from thy meat offering. With all thy offering thou shalt offer salt."(Leviticus 2:13) One may wonder why God said he would bring me out of the salt, and why everyone must be sprinkled with it.

Let's investigate what salt is and what it's used for in everyday life to help you discover God's meaning. "Salt is used for preserving and seasoning, it's an ingredient that gives savor, which means having a distinctive quality. It also gives flavor, which means full of life and vigor, it also gives pungency, which means sharpness of wit. It's used as an aperient, which is a laxative, and a catharsis, which means to cleanse or purge." Sin is ingrained deep within the character of man, and that's why everyone must be sprinkled in God's salt. Suffering, trials and affliction is the salt God uses to bring forth the characteristics of salting, and enduring the salt is the price one has to pay for heaven. Persecution is a supreme order from God, it is ordained for every life pursuing heaven, that's why many are deterred from walking this road. God's salting is a callous process, its Divine results far outweigh the purging cries and pains of your human emotions. The salting at times is so unbearable, you may feel that God

The Road To Paradise

is against you due to the crushing he allows to make you whole. The God of salting is unfamiliar to the world, but the pure are close to him. Because sin is an alien characteristic to the creation of man and not human, but has a supernatural origin, its power easily enslaved humanity. Sin is rebellious, undisciplined, blinding, and perverse and its nature has saturated the world for centuries and made it hard to tell the difference between what's natural and what's sin. The reason why God made the Ten Commandments was so that man would know right from wrong, and be made accountable for his sins. The Ten Commandments wasn't God's solution to sin, it was the exposing of sin. The conquering of sin can never be obtained by human abilities, its inhuman origin requires a supernatural purging and sin's resistance makes the salting process long and painful. Suffering is admirable and highly honored in heaven, because it's a condition you accept when submitting to God's will. *"By faith Moses, when he was come to years, refused to be called the son of Pharaoh's daughter, choosing rather to suffer affliction with the people of God, than to enjoy the pleasures of sin for a season."(Hebrews 11:24-25)* There are great pleasures in sin, unbridled pleasures that appeal to what we feel is natural. Sin uses lust and passion to control our reason, comforts us by giving us sinful desires, and justifies a lie, if it makes us feel better.

Sin is so deep that it has disguised itself as man's natural feeling, to the extent he will fight to keep the sin within him alive. The results of sin are complete in devastation and destruction, because it has and knows no closure, its endless world of false security, deception, and sexual perversion keeps him contained in a circle of human decay. The salt of God attacks the results of sin, it uncovers and exposes its deepest strongholds, and weeds and sifts out sin's attributes. Sin brought death into the world. Disease, perversion, and everything that opposes God, sin is responsible for. God is holy, holy is a consuming fire that is impossible to stand before unsalted. This fire is the salt that destroys all evil, and its terrifying pureness is impalpable. *"For our God is a consuming fire."(Hebrews 12:29)* In this life there is no preparation more grievous, and no results more highly honored, than from the salting of God. *"Now no chastening for the present seemeth to be joyous, but afterwards it yieldeth the peaceable fruit of righteous unto them which are exercised thereby."(Hebrews 12:11)* He who is salted is he who walks closest to God, in the high place far above the titles and positions of man, the salting allows you to understand God's character as you become more like Him. God loves humanity, and He wants to bless and care for you, but because of His holiness it's impossible for Him to over look your sin and evil, to be a part of your life. God has been trying to reach man ever since He lost them to sin, the problem is that man is not in his first state of perfection, when it was easy for God to commune with him, and not worry about the fire of His holiness consuming them for their unsavouriness.

Adam, the first man, was a perfect man without sin in his origin, and knew no evil. He was made for God's pleasure and everything God made in the earth was for him to enjoy and have dominion over. *"Man in his origin was made to be just like God."(Gen 1:28)* "Let us make man in our image. After our likeness."(Gen 1:26) The whole purpose to God's salting is to get you back to your first state of perfection, so that God can walk with you, talk with you, and give you dominion and blessings in your life. Sin took away the divinity of man's first state. He lost the characteristics of God and put on the characteristics of sin. He lost his alliance with the family of heaven and fell out of fellowship with God. Man was alone in the world, without divinity, without the power to withstand sin, and after some time, man had no knowledge of his first state, because sin flourished in the world until there was no evidence of his divinity. *"And God saw that the wickedness of man was great in the earth, and that every imagination of the thoughts of his heart was only evil continually."(Gen 6:5)*

It was a great disappointment to God that man no longer desired His presence, nor wanted His companionship, but would rather worship evil and enjoy the perversions of sin. Sin had become so powerful that God lost all man to it, the whole world was corrupt and only one man out of the whole world was righteous. *"And God looked upon the earth and behold, it was corrupt, for all flesh had corrupted his way upon the earth."(Gen 6:12)* "One should consider the power of sin when only one man out of the whole world escaped its corruption. Herein we see the character of God. He lost everyone in the world to sin and then destroyed the world, but then valued the righteousness of one man so highly that He built a new world around him. God is not concerned with numbers. He already knows that only a remnant of people will follow righteousness. So God decided that He would choose one people in the earth to be His people, and they would become witnesses to the rest of the world that He was alive. *"But thou, Israel, art my servant, Jacob whom I have chosen, the seed of Abraham my friend."(Isaiah 41:8)* *"Ye are my witness, saith the Lord, and my servant whom I have chosen, that you may know and believe me."(Isaiah 43:10)* God chose the Hebrew people, the Jews, to be the light of the world and the apple of His eye. And for them he would come down to earth and perform miracles for their protection and show mighty signs of His power.

God wanted the rest of the world to crave for the God of the Jews, and the personal attention He gave to them. But sin was a problem in these chosen people also and God decided to deal with them. "Behold, I have refined thee, but not with silver, I have chosen thee in the furnace of affliction." In order for the Jews to be an example of how He wanted humanity, He would first have to purge the sin in His chosen people. And the salting began. One must understand that everyone chosen must be salted. The Jews have always been a people plagued by great hardships, because hardships bring about submission to God and acknowledgment of sin. The Jews had been oppressed and made slaves in Egypt for four hundred years, until their cries reached and overloaded heaven. God did deliver them from Egypt, with great signs and wonders, and was leading them to their own land. Now this is what I want to speak about. Egypt, the wilderness, and the promise land, is a Biblical depiction of man's plight from sin to salvation. If man has been in slavery and bondage for hundreds of years, and all of a sudden is set free, the characteristics of being enslaved are still within him. Even though he is free. All he knows is how to be a slave, and this is exactly how it is when you're enslaved to sin. As a slave you don't know the first thing about freedom. You don't know what your rights are, or what belongs to you as a free person. A slave is taught to be dependent upon their oppressors, to take on their ways and submit to their ideas. Even though God delivered the children of Israel from bondage, their actions and reactions to God were like a slave, and thus God chose the wilderness for their salting. What would have taken three days to get to their promise land, took forty years because they were still slaves to their old ways. The salt of God breaks the yoke of a slave mentality, which is the inability of man to believe he can have better, reaching back to the comfort of his old ways, and the conditioning of self-hate. Sin is the Egypt in man's life, and unless man is sprinkled in God's salt, he can't go to the promise land, only back to slavery in Egypt.

In my sleep God spoke to me: "Be careful, the Devil will try to get you through your self-esteem."

Satan is the opposer of righteousness, the accuser of God's people, and the corrupter of the world. I've been where Satan stays. He lives in the house of sexual perversion and idols, he has monuments of decadence built in his honor, and millions of dollars for people who continue his advancement. And we as Christians must stand back to back, and shoulder to shoulder, and help

The Road To Paradise

the weaker Christians to withstand and resist him. The forgiveness of sins is the hammer that God uses to break the power of Satan's yoke upon your life, and accepting Jesus as your Savior gives you the power to leave Satan's house despite the power he uses to keep you there. I have encountered Satan in dreams on many occasions in my life. These appearances were allowances of God, not for Satan's benefit, but for me to understand what God has allowed him to know about me, and his limitations in my life.

I was sixteen at the time of the first dream. Satan was before me. I didn't see his physical appearance but I knew him by his presence. He said to me "Andre your going down, I'm going to give you a bad name and a bad reputation." I then ran from him to the presence of God and told God what Satan said he was going to do to me, God spoke to me and said "Andre not so, you're different, you go all the way to the end of a situation, then I fill you up again." This dream was to assure me of God's sovereignty in my life, despite any situation I go through. The dream also gave me insight into my future, but at sixteen I couldn't understand the fullness of this dream, or understand it was an outline of my whole life. The fact that Satan said he would give me a bad name and reputation showed that there were going to be some situations I go through that wouldn't show me in a good light. But God said I was different-I would go all the way to the end of the situation, then He would fill me up again. Meaning that the situation had purpose, and that there was something ordained for me to learn and understand with each situation Satan tried to use to destroy me. And once I understood what God wanted me to learn, he would defeat the situation and prepare me for the next. And for the next twenty years from, 16 to 36 years old, this is exactly how my life went.

In another dream, I was walking down the street and there were people all around who were demon possessed, and as I walked past them the demons would come out of the people because God's power was so strong on me. Then I got on this bus full of people, and this man came up to me, who wasn't just possessed but was Satan himself, and said "from since the beginning of the time, I've never seen God in such a violent manner that I see Him in you." "And from the days of John the Baptist until the present time, the kingdom of heaven has endured violence, and violent men seize it by force (as a precious prize-a share in the heavenly kingdom is sought with most ardent zeal and intense exertion)."(Matt 11:11 Amp) God wanted me to know that I was different, so much so that even Satan was in awe that God had manifested something different in me that he hadn't seen from God in man. This allowed me to understand the mind of God a little more clearly concerning the affairs of mankind. That the stigma we associate with mistakes are governed by a higher power, and judged within Divine purpose when you're chosen. *"Then Ananias answered, Lord, I have heard by many of this man, how much evil he has done to thy saints at Jerusalem. But the Lord said unto him, go thy way: for he is a chosen vessel unto me."(Acts 9:13&15)* The apostle Paul understood this after his conversion, and I was shown it before the Road to Paradise began, because I needed to understand that what I would go through was for a purpose. The tragedy of my situations would never engulf me, but spur me to press to the end of them, because I knew consolation was there. This consciousness developed a defiance and spiritual violence in me that produced such a resistance not to bow-that any situation or circumstance that life or Satan brought my way was viewed as minuscule-because I had been prepared for whatever. It didn't matter to me how many mistakes I made, how many pits I fell in, how big or threatening a problem was, or who pointed the finger at me, I would never stop, and would charge against perilous situations and miracles would happen, because I believed that the power of God, was more powerful than the power of the Devil.

Chapter Six: The Revelation of Paradise

In my sleep God spoke to me: "I'm not mad at you for all your past sins and mistakes, but I will put you in a high place, and one day you will cry and break, like you never have before, when you think about all the things I brought you through."

In Seattle, when I was 19 years old, I was going to this church and had a dream. In the dream Jesus appeared in the church, and the people in the congregation began coming to the Lord, telling Him their problems and petitioning Him. In the dream the Lord was very disappointed and hurt by this, because the people didn't realize that they were in the presence of God. And that in the presence of God, there are no needs, no cares, and no wants. This dream was the beginning of me understanding the revelation, the necessity, and the power of being in God's presence. But it wasn't until I was thirty-six, with twenty years of developmental experiences, under the salting of God, that I received a breakthrough and complete understanding of the revelation. What God was showing me was that Providence, supernatural provision and action, is being in His presence. Its not enough to know the information, you have to believe through living the information. You must understand that there is nothing more important in existence, time or eternity, than being in God's presence; it is the ultimate objective and achievement.

And Jesus' death was for you to have access to God's presence again. Being that this is true, why hasn't this been our main focus? Because like in my dream, we don't know what it fully entails when we're fully engulfed in God's presence. When God gave me the dream I was a believer that prayer changes things, but I didn't understand how and why it works, because at the time, I didn't have enough experience walking with God to comprehend the language of the level I hadn't arrived at yet. I didn't know the extent of His realness and abilities on a personal level until I engaged life with Him. The mountains and obstacles were the proving ground, and it was in darkness and despair that we became inseparable. I understood after the breakthrough that it was the attitude of being in His presence that made the difference. In my beginning, at age sixteen, my walk with God birthed trust, intimacy, deep love, longing and neediness for God. I knew Him, and the years I had walked with Him, gave me eyes to understand that the revelation was being in God's presence as part of the heavenly family within Him, and not someone outside of His care petitioning Him as a stranger. This revelation is a spur to pray, to walk with God and submit to his salting for the next level, the high place in God's presence that is appointed to the twenty-four Elders in heaven, where there are no human needs, cares or wants. "The earnest (heartfelt, continued) prayer of a righteous man makes tremendous power available (dynamic in working)."(James 5:16Amp) What I understood from my breakthrough was that I didn't just have access to power like before, but that I was power and that being in prayer (His presence) within Him, activated it. "For he that is entered into his rest, he also hath ceased from his own works, as God did from his."(Hebrews 4:10) Once I was within Him in prayer (His presence) my care didn't require words of petition. The transition made me live in the consciousness of his Divine perfectness, and the completeness of me being there made the thought of my care obsolete. "But you, beloved, build yourselves up (Founded) on your most holy faith, (Make progress, rise like an edifice higher and higher), praying in the holy spirit."(Jude 1:20Amp) It is here where I understood how the human person embodies God, and walks, and lives in the supernatural-it is the consciousness of God's active presence in every area and happening in your life. When prayer (His presence) is no longer a duty but a desire, when it's understood as the most important organ in the spiritual body, your most holy faith, when all of life's activities become a far and distant second, and your existence becomes validated within it, only then will you know who God is. The central theme in the Christian walk is dying to self, which is the sacrifice of one's will and desires. And the reason why most people will never know who God is, is because they refuse His chastisement. "Who led thee through the great and terrible wilderness, wherein were fiery serpents, and scorpions, and drought, where there was no water, who brought the forth water out of the rock of flint; who fed thee in the wilderness with manna, which thy fathers knew not, that he might humble thee, and that he might prove thee, to do thee good at thy latter end."(Deut 8:15&16) You will never know who God is with just a walk in the park, you have to walk with Him through the valley of the shadow of death, so that he can show you that He's bigger than death, bigger than life, and bigger than all things that exist. Bask in God's presence! Which means: "relax in warmth and light, and derive great pleasure from it." I'm trying to make you understand that there's a place within God (His presence) where the works (power, miracles) Jesus said we'd do greater than Him, becomes yours. The problem with the Christian walk today is that the believer is too busy trying to live. But while God wants you to be busy dying, you have placed all your efforts on talents, abilities, gifts…and are busy doing the work. God wants the church to relinquish the work of their human efforts,\ and refocus them only on prayer (His presence) so that the age of supernatural care can be brought down. "Not by might, nor by power, but by my spirit saith the Lord of host."(Zech 4:6) Remember, it's the attitude of being in His presence that makes the difference, knowing who you are within Him, and understanding the attitude, and the awesomeness of God that comes from time with Him. If you have worked, pressed, strived and possess all things that are humanly possible in this world, you haven't even achieved a first step the moment you have come into the world of God's presence. Prayer (His presence) is not a punishment, its Paradise!

Thus says the Lord of host: if you will walk in My ways and keep My charge, then also you shall rule My house and have charge of My courts, and I will give you access (To My presence) and places to walk among these who stand here. (Zech 3:7) Amp.

Chapter Seven: The Angel, The Future and Hell

The Road To Paradise

I was seventeen and had been living at a shelter for three weeks in downtown Seattle. We could sleep there, but when the morning came we had to leave. I walked around downtown, as I'd done for the past three weeks. As I was walking, there was a black man talking to himself, I could see and slightly hear him from a distance. The closer he came I began to try to listen to what he was saying. And when he got close to me I listened real close. He was quoting a verse from the Bible. I knew because I had read it before. He ways saying, "I rather go the way of a bear robbed of her whelps than go the way of a fool." I turned and said to him, "All a fool needs is love just like everyone else." When I said that, the man looked into my eyes and said, "God has chosen you to be the shepherd over his sheep, you've gone as low as you can go and it's only up from here. Moses brought the Law, but you will bring God's love. It's not going to be easy, it's going to be real hard. But one day you're going to have a beautiful family, and when you come, they will know it because they will see it in your eyes. And one day you will tell this story, and no matter where you are, one day I will see you again." I was speechless because he had told me things that only God and I knew, and he kept saying to me, "ask me, ask me," but I was scared to ask him how he knew about those things, so I asked him his name, he said it was James, and he repeated, "ask me," and when he knew I was to overwhelmed, he said to me, "What I have was given to me to give to you and I've waited to give it to you." I asked him where does he live, he said, "downtown," smiled and walked away, I've never seen him again.

"Be not forgetful to entertain strangers, for thereby some have entertained angels unawares."(Hebrews 13:2)

It was in March of 1999. I was in jail and God showed me the future in a dream. I was shown that in twenty years from the time of the dream, at Christmas time, God will cause a star to fall from the sky into the water on earth. Hell from beneath will be opened up unto the earth, fire will be everywhere, and people will want to flee from the fire on the land by water, but the star that fell into the water made the water hotter than the land. Everything was very dark from the smoke from under the earth, so that there was no light. This is supposed to happen in the year 2019.

"And a fifth angel sounded, and I saw a star fall from heaven unto the earth, and to him was given the key of the bottomless pit. And he opened the bottomless pit, and there arose a smoke out the pit, the smoke of a great furnace; and the sun and the air were

darkened by reason of the smoke of the pit."(Rev 9:1-2)

It was also in March of 1999 that God showed me about hell in a dream. In the dream God showed me that Hell wasn't just one place, that hell was many countries underneath the earth. The first country is called Appollus, and it is the size of the earth. The people that go to Appollus, are those who receive the most lenient punishment. The Punishment in Appollus is loneliness, for Appollus is a country of Hell where people are confined to a place all by themselves run by computers or machines, never being able to see, hear or talk to another human being for eternity. I also saw bigger countries underneath Appollus, and smaller countries underneath the bigger ones. And the further down the country you were in, the worse it was. In the dream, I was afraid to go down and look into the other countries because the ugly and evil in those countries was more than I could comprehend or bear. In the dream, I looked and beheld all existence, heaven, earth, and the countries of hell, and everything put together looked like the shape of a big chicken. Earth was the belly, heaven was the head, and hell, with all its countries made up the legs that went all the way down to its feet. And the countries that were down at the feet were exceedingly and horribly evil, and the pain there was a pain that doesn't exist in the earth-something so terrible I dreaded to even look at the country. *"For a fire is kindled in mine anger, and shall burn unto the lowest hell."(Deut 32:22*

> *"Hear now My words: If there is a prophet among you, I the Lord make Myself known to him in a vision and speak to him in a dream."(Numbers 12:6)Amp.*
> ***

About the Author

André Taylor was on his own at 16. He was ordained as a minister at age 18. He became a pimp at age 23– by 30 he was in Federal prison. Six months after being released from prison, he was invited to lecture at U.N.L.V. University, which he accepted several times. He is now married, an entrepeneur and continues to lecture at college campuses. André Taylor lives in Los Angeles, where he heads his new movement, *Streetsweeper Ministries*.

Visit us online at http://www.streetsweeperministries.com
Andretaylor@streetsweeperministries.com

Made in the USA
Columbia, SC
02 June 2020